CANADA

BY
WILLIAM ANTHONY

BookLife
PUBLISHING

©2019
BookLife Publishing Ltd.
King's Lynn
Norfolk PE30 4LS
All rights reserved.
Printed in Malaysia.

A catalogue record for this book is available from the British Library.

ISBN: 978-1-78637-687-9

Written by:
William Anthony

Edited by:
Emilie Dufresne

Designed by:
Gareth Liddington

Photocredits:

Cover – Abihatsira Issac, KikoStock, grop, lookus, piyaphong, DiViArt, Veja, Natasha Breen, Studio KIWI, Victoria43, 4 – Tupungato, BobNoah, RomanR, 5 – Perre Leclerc, Daxiao Productions, 6 – Wangkun Jia, Kit Leong, 7 – Wangkun Jia, Ferenz, 8 – EQRoy, GreenArt, almaje, 9 – Habib Sajid, Dr. Suleman Merchant, Marc Bruxelle, Brent Hofacker, 10 – Andriy Blokhin, Denis Roger, StockMediaSeller, 11 – Kiev Victor, Ronnie Chua, 12 – Thomas Brissiaud, Africa Studio, Oliay, Adisa, 13 – Vlad G, Bob Hilscher, Neamov, 14 – Kiev.Victor, SAHAS2015, W. Phokin, nexus 7, Mykola Kutsyi, DeymousHR, Paulo Vilela, 15 – CPQ, Canicula, Facto Photo, 16 – Roman Babakin, Lidiia Kozhevnikova, 17 – Henryk Sadura, GTS Productions, cherezoff, marekuliasz, 18 – Allna Reynbakh, Art Babych, 19 – bmszealand, Bing Wen, 20 – Sophia Granchinho, sirtravelalot, Mr Z, 21 – AndreAnita, Daniil Ermolchuk, 22 – Zhukova Valentyna, Martin M303, TungCheung, pukach, 23 – Brie Robertson, R.M.Nunes, Cagkan Sayin, Aleksandra Suzi, 24 – EB Adventure Photography, Robert Nyholm, komkrit Preechachanwate, Grushin, 25 – Sebastien Launay, Sergei Backlakov, Iasha, 26 – A. Michael Brown, Jukka Jantunen, Tsugliev, 27 – Pi-Lens, 29 – Evgeny Turaev, 30 – Brent Hofacker, Pi-Lens.

Images are courtesy of Shutterstock.com. With thanks to Getty Images, Thinkstock Photo and iStockphoto.

All facts, statistics, web addresses and URLs in this book were verified as valid and accurate at time of writing. No responsibility for any changes to external websites or references can be accepted by either the author or publisher.

CONTENTS

Page 4   Welcome to Canada

Page 6   Québec City

Page 8   La Poutine Week

Page 10   Notre-Dame Basilica
          of Montréal

Page 12   Rideau Canal

Page 14   CN Tower

Page 16   Niagara Falls

Page 18   Manito Ahbee Festival

Page 20   Animal Spotting

Page 22   Banff National Park

Page 24   Vancouver Canucks

Page 26   Aurora Borealis

Page 28   The Journey

Page 30   Au Revoir

Page 31   Glossary

Page 32   Index

Words that look like
this can be found
in the glossary
on page 31.

WELCOME TO CANADA

Bonjour! That means hello in French. Don't worry, you're in the right country – I'm from Saint John in Canada. We speak both English and French in this city. My name is Remy.

Look out for coordinates in boxes like these. Use the internet to explore these places online. You can ask an adult to help you.

CANADA IS THE SECOND-BIGGEST COUNTRY IN THE WORLD.

ROAD TRIP

My family and I are taking a trip across our home country of Canada. There are a lot of long journeys between our stops, but it will be worth it to see everything!

SAINT JOHN IS IN NEW BRUNSWICK.

THE LANDSCAPE

In Canada, we have big cities, snowy mountains, thick forests and frozen Arctic regions. Not many countries can say that!

I CAN'T WAIT TO VISIT ALL THE DIFFERENT PARTS OF CANADA!

Our country is best known for its beautiful landscapes, where you can find lots of weird and wonderful animals, as well as our maple trees. Over Almost three-quarters of the world's maple syrup is made in Canada.

MAPLE SYRUP COMES FROM MAPLE TREES. IT TASTES REALLY GOOD WITH PANCAKES.

QUÉBEC CITY

First, we headed to Québec City in the <u>province</u> of Québec, which is next to my home province of New Brunswick. We have come here to learn about Canada's relationship with France.

THE ST. LAWRENCE RIVER WAS VERY IMPORTANT IN HELPING THE FRENCH TO <u>COLONISE</u> QUÉBEC.

NEW FRANCE

Canada became influenced by French <u>culture</u> over 500 years ago. Some parts of Canada still use the French language today. In 1534, a French <u>navigator</u> called Jacques Cartier claimed part of Québec in the name of France, calling it New France.

QUÉBEC CITY WASN'T FOUNDED UNTIL LATER, IN 1608.

FRENCH TRADITIONS

When the French settled in Québec City, they brought lots of French <u>traditions</u> with them. New France used French laws, the French language, and brought <u>Roman Catholicism</u> to Canada.

THE NOTRE-DAME-DES-VICTOIRES CHURCH IN QUÉBEC CITY IS A ROMAN CATHOLIC CHURCH.

QUÉBEC CITY TODAY

I've been able to speak to people in French while we've been in Québec City. French is still the official language of the Québec province. I've enjoyed learning about where my country's French culture came from.

THIS IS A STATUE OF THE FOUNDER OF QUÉBEC CITY, SAMUEL DE CHAMPLAIN.

LA POUTINE WEEK

Canada is famous for a lot of things, and food is one of them. We've come to Montréal for a week-long celebration of one of Québec's favourite dishes – la poutine.

MONTRÉAL HAS THE LARGEST POPULATION OF ANY CITY IN QUÉBEC, AND THE SECOND-LARGEST IN CANADA.

FRIES, FRIES AND MORE FRIES

Poutine is a dish with lots of fries topped with gravy and cheese curds. It can look rather messy, but it tastes delicious! During La Poutine Week, restaurants make fancy versions of the dish.

SOME PEOPLE BELIEVE THAT THE WORD POUTINE ROUGHLY TRANSLATES AS 'HOT MESS'!

MESSY PAST

I asked lots of people if they knew where poutine actually came from, but no one was sure. Apparently, lots of different towns and cities in Québec claim to be the place it was first made.

No matter where it's from, we've had so much poutine since we arrived that we can hardly walk!

MAPLE TREE

MAPLE SYRUP

The food that we're maybe even more famous for is maple syrup. We make maple syrup from the <u>sap</u> in maple trees. When you boil the sap, you end up with our famous maple syrup.

MAPLE SAP BEING COLLECTED

NOTRE-DAME BASILICA OF MONTRÉAL

While we were still in Montréal, we went to visit a famous piece of Roman Catholic history in the province of Québec. In the old part of Montréal you can see the Notre-Dame Basilica.

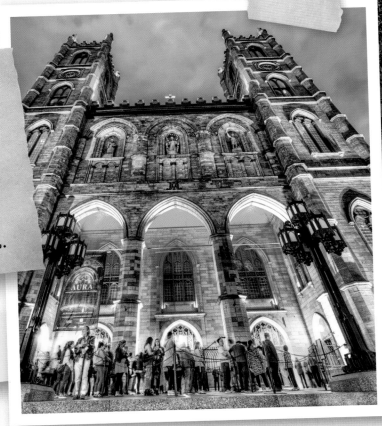

NOTRE-DAME'S TOWERS ARE VERY TALL!

The Notre-Dame Basilica of Montréal was one of the first churches in Canada to be built in a style called Gothic Revival. It was designed by an architect from New York, USA, called James O'Donnell and was built between 1824 and 1829.

GOTHIC REVIVAL

The Gothic Revival was a period when architects started designing in the Gothic style again. Gothic buildings are usually made from stone, have tall and pointed spires, detailed sculptures, large glass windows and a pointed arch.

POINTED SPIRES

NOTRE-DAME BASILICA OF MONTRÉAL COORDINATES:
45.5045,
-73.5561

The <u>basilica</u> is just as impressive on the inside as it is on the outside. My favourite part of visiting the basilica was hearing the hymns being played on the organ.

RIDEAU CANAL
BRRR!

Winters in Canada are some of the coldest in the world. In some parts of Canada, temperatures can drop to around -30 degrees Celsius (°C). We've travelled to Canada's capital city of Ottawa to have fun in the cold weather.

ICE SKATING

OTTAWA LOOKS LIKE A FAIRY-TALE CITY IN THE WINTER.

One of the best-known parts of our Canadian culture is ice skating, and we take to rinks to skate for fun throughout the year. Ice hockey is one of our most popular sports. It's similar to ordinary hockey but we play it on ice rinks.

GRAB YOUR SKATES!

FROZEN OVER

Winters in Ottawa are an <u>average</u> of -10°C, which means lots of things freeze over, including the Rideau Canal. Because it stays frozen all winter long, everyone comes here to ice skate.

SO MANY PEOPLE HAD COME TO SKATE.

Because 7.8 kilometres of the canal freezes over, it has been declared the record holder for the largest naturally frozen ice rink in the world. Dad tried his best at skating, but the longest he stayed standing for was about eight seconds. Poor Dad!

THE CANAL ICE RINK IS THE SAME SIZE AS 90 OLYMPIC-SIZE SKATING RINKS PUT TOGETHER.

CN TOWER

WE CAME HERE TO SEE THIS.

Next we went to Toronto. Both Toronto and Ottawa are in the province of Ontario. Toronto is the most-populated city in Canada — even bigger than our capital city.

THE CN TOWER IS 553 METRES TALL.

CN TOWER COORDINATES: 43.6426, -79.3871

HIGH IN THE SKY

Toronto has lots of very tall towers in the city centre. Lots of them are owned by businesses or are hotels. But there are none taller than the famous CN Tower.

14

I learned all about the history of the tower when we visited it. It took almost three and a half years to build and was opened in 1976. It cost 63 million Canadian dollars to build.

There are lots of things you can do at the top of the tower. We took a walk on the glass floor. You can see all the way down to the ground. It was a bit scary at first.

THIS IS A PHOTO I TOOK OF THE VIEW.

YOU CAN HOOK INTO A SAFETY HARNESS AND GO FOR A WALK AT THE TOP. THE HARNESS EVEN LETS YOU LEAN OVER THE EDGE!

NIAGARA FALLS

With our feet safely back on the ground, we headed to one of the most impressive natural sights in Canada. Not all of it is in Canada – most of it is in the USA.

WE WENT TO SEE NIAGARA FALLS.

We still stayed in Canada while we went to see the huge waterfalls. Two of the three waterfalls are just across the border in the USA, but the best views are on our side of the river.

THE THREE FALLS

There are three sets of waterfalls on the Niagara River. They are the American Falls, the Bridal Veil Falls and the Canadian Falls, which are also known as the Horseshoe Falls. The waterfalls are over 12,000 years old.

AMERICAN FALLS   BRIDAL VEIL FALLS   CANADIAN FALLS

ELECTRICITY

The waterfalls are used to make electricity. Both New York in the USA and the province of Ontario in Canada use power stations that make electricity from the flow of the water.

THE ELECTRICITY MADE FROM THE RIVER MAKES UP FOR AROUND ONE-QUARTER OF THE POWER SUPPLY OF NEW YORK AND ONTARIO.

ON THE USA SIDE, YOU CAN EVEN WALK UP CLOSE TO THE WATERFALLS IN THE CAVE OF THE WINDS.

MANITO AHBEE FESTIVAL

We headed for Winnipeg next. Winnipeg is in the province of Manitoba. My parents said that this was one of the most important parts of the journey.

WE WENT TO WINNIPEG TO LEARN ABOUT <u>INDIGENOUS</u> PEOPLES.

THE INDIGENOUS CANADIANS

The term Indigenous peoples is used to describe First Nations, Métis and Inuit peoples. These are the original groups of people that lived in Canada. These communities still exist today.

FIRST NATIONS DANCERS

THE FESTIVAL

The Manito Ahbee Festival celebrates Indigenous culture every year. The festival is started by the lighting of the sacred fire and a traditional friendship dance to welcome everybody.

DANCING AND MUSIC MAKE UP A BIG PART OF INDIGENOUS FESTIVALS.

There is a part of the festival called Youth Education Day. I learned a lot about my country's past during it. My favourite part was hearing the Inuit throat singing.

INUIT THROAT SINGING INVOLVES TWO PEOPLE FACING EACH OTHER AND USING THEIR THROATS TO MAKE MUSICAL SOUNDS.

19

ANIMAL SPOTTING

Canada is home to lots of very cool and unusual animals. I live in a city so I haven't seen many cool animals. We headed to the province of Nunavut, where I got to see some of them.

THIS IS ARVIAT, WHERE WE WENT TO SEE THE ANIMALS.

TRADITIONAL CLOTHING

ARVIAT

Arviat is found on the coast of Hudson Bay and is home to an Inuit community. People travel here to see lots of different animals.

IT WAS VERY INTERESTING TO LEARN ABOUT THE INUIT PEOPLE IN WINNIPEG AND HOW THEY LIVE.

POLAR BEARS

One of the main reasons that lots of people visit Arviat is to see the polar bears during their yearly <u>migration</u>. We got on a small plane in search of some polar bears and we found a big one walking in the snow.

BELUGA WHALES

Arviat is by the coast of Hudson Bay, so we were able to take a fun trip out on a boat in search of beluga whales. One of them came up to our boat to say bonjour!

BANFF NATIONAL PARK

For the next part of our trip, we went to Banff National Park. A national park is an area of land that is protected by a <u>government</u> because of how beautiful or important it is.

THE ROCKIES

Banff National Park is one of four national parks located in the famous mountain range called the Canadian Rockies. The Rockies can be found along part of the border between the Alberta and British Columbia provinces.

THE THREE OTHER NATIONAL PARKS THAT ARE PART OF THE ROCKIES ARE JASPER, YOHO AND KOOTENAY.

SKIING

We started high up in the Canadian Rockies. We went to the Lake Louise Ski Resort where my family and I learned to ski.

DAD WASN'T VERY GOOD ON THE ICE IN OTTAWA, BUT HE WAS REALLY GOOD AT SKIING!

CANOEING

There are lots of other things to do in Banff National Park. We went to the crystal-blue Moraine Lake to try canoeing. Canoeing involves two people paddling at the same time in a long, narrow boat, called a canoe.

MUM WAS THE BEST AT CANOEING; DAD COULDN'T WORKOUT HOW TO STEER!

VANCOUVER CANUCKS

We were very tired after all that exercise in Banff National Park. We decided that we would watch other people do some exercise instead, so we went to watch some ice hockey.

WE CAME TO VANCOUVER TO WATCH THE CANUCKS PLAY. YOU CAN'T MISS THEIR STADIUM.

ICE HOCKEY

We Canadians love ice hockey – it is a national sport. Ice hockey is played with two teams of six players on an ice rink, using hockey sticks to try and hit a small, round and flat puck into the other team's goal.

ICE HOCKEY TEAMS FROM THE USA AND CANADA PLAY AGAINST EACH OTHER IN A COMPETITION CALLED THE NHL (NATIONAL HOCKEY LEAGUE).

PUCK

THE CANUCKS

The Vancouver Canucks are one of seven Canadian teams in the NHL. Their home stadium is called the Rogers Arena and that's where we saw them play.

THE STADIUM WAS PACKED!

OLYMPIC VILLAGE

While we were still in Vancouver, we thought we should visit the Olympic Village, which was built for the 2010 Winter Olympics. Vancouver was the host city for the Games and you can still use the venues today.

AURORA BOREALIS

I can't believe the trip has gone so quickly. I was really excited about our journey to Yukon. We went to see something I'd only ever seen in photos — the northern lights!

MANY OF THE PEOPLE OF YUKON HAVE FIRST NATIONS HERITAGE. I'M GLAD I LEARNED ABOUT THIS AT THE MANITO AHBEE FESTIVAL.

YUKON

Yukon is found at the northwest of Canada. It is an area that is full of open land, mountains, lakes and wildlife. In fact, the number of four-legged animals is far greater than the number of humans.

WE GOT TO SEE A MOOSE AS WE TRAVELLED THROUGH YUKON.

AURORAS

We came to see the aurora borealis. This is a light show that appears in the sky, caused by <u>charged particles</u> from the Sun entering our planet's <u>atmosphere</u>.

WHAT AN ENDING!

We headed out into the wilderness and lay in the snow together to watch the lights. They were even more beautiful than in the photos. This has been a perfect way to end our trip across Canada.

THE AURORA BOREALIS IS SOMETIMES CALLED THE NORTHERN LIGHTS.

THE JOURNEY

Look at all the places we have visited on our journey.

WOW – THIS WAS BREATHTAKING!

AURORA BOREALIS

VANCOUVER CANUCKS

BANFF NATIONAL PARK

MANITO AHBEE FESTIVAL

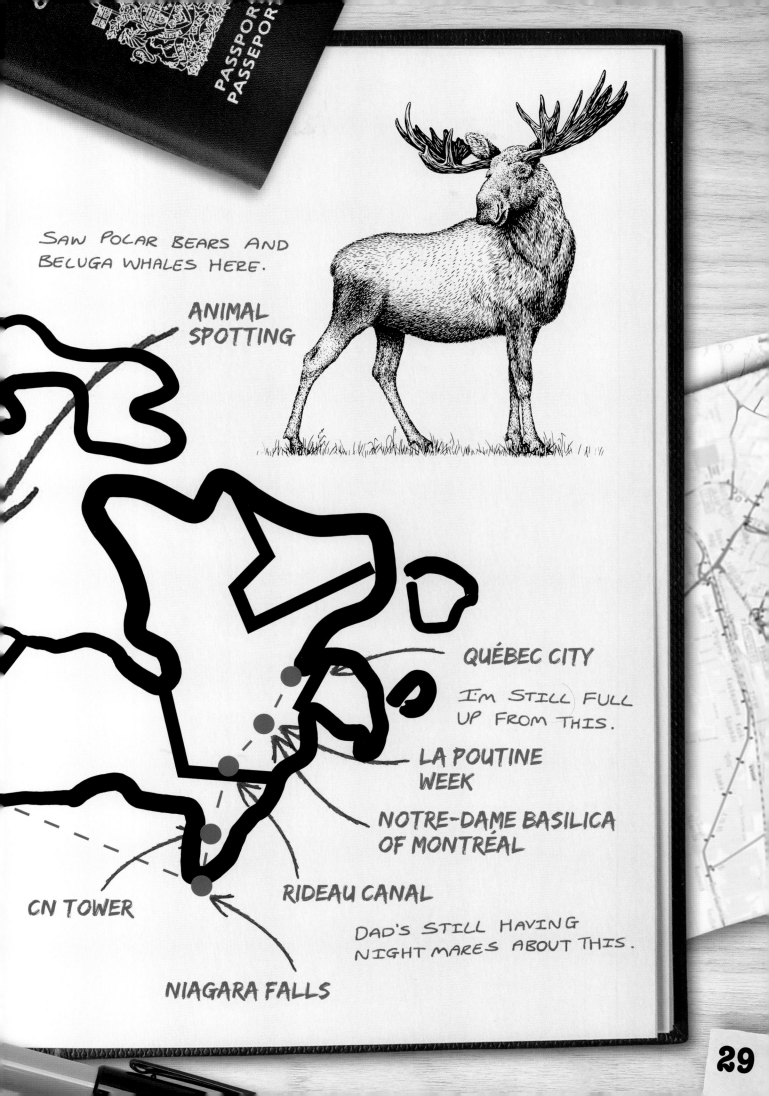

SAW POLAR BEARS AND BELUGA WHALES HERE.

ANIMAL SPOTTING

QUÉBEC CITY

I'M STILL FULL UP FROM THIS.

LA POUTINE WEEK

NOTRE-DAME BASILICA OF MONTRÉAL

RIDEAU CANAL

DAD'S STILL HAVING NIGHTMARES ABOUT THIS.

CN TOWER

NIAGARA FALLS

AU REVOIR

It's time to say au revoir, which means goodbye in French. I've had an incredible time exploring my country with my family. I learned so much about the people, places, animals and food in Canada.

My favourite part of the trip has to be the last part – seeing the northern lights. I still have one big question after this trip: will Dad ever stay standing up on ice for more than eight seconds?

GLOSSARY

architect	a person who designs buildings
atmosphere	the mixture of gases that makes up the air and surrounds the Earth
average	the typical amount or most central number of a range of numbers
basilica	a building that is a type of Roman Catholic church
charged particles	very small bits of matter that have an electrical charge
colonise	to move to a new land and take control of the area and people
culture	the traditions, ideas and ways of life of a particular group of people
curds	thick substances that form when milk turns sour, used to make cheese
government	the group of people that run a country and decide its laws
heritage	things that are inherited from earlier generations such as traits, language and buildings
Indigenous	originating or naturally found in a particular place
migration	seasonal movements of animals from one region to another
navigator	a person who finds out or knows how to get to a place
population	the number of people living in a place
province	any one of the large parts that some countries are divided into
Roman Catholicism	a type of Christian religion
sap	liquid that carries water and nutrients to the parts of a plant
traditions	ways of doing something that have been used by a particular group for a long time

INDEX

A
Arctic 5

B
beluga whales 12, 29

C
Canadian Rockies 22–23

E
electricity 17

F
food
- maple syrup 5, 9
- pancakes 5
- poutine 8–9, 29

G
Gothic Revival 10–11

I
ice hockey 12, 24–25
ice skating 12–13
Indigenous peoples
- First Nations 18–19, 26
- Inuit 18–20
Métis 18–19

M
Manitoba 18–19, 29
moose 26

N
national parks 22–24, 28
NHL 24–25
Nunavut 20–21, 29

O
Ontario 14–17, 29

P
polar bears 21, 29

R
Roman Catholic 7, 10

Y
Yukon 26–27, 29